Figure Painting

Applied to

Architecture

AN ADDRESS DELIVERED BY

FREDERIC CROWNINSHIELD

BEFORE THE

Architectural League

OF NEW YORK

November 5th, 1888

In the interest of creating a more extensive selection of rare historical book reprints, we have chosen to reproduce this title even though it may possibly have occasional imperfections such as missing and blurred pages, missing text, poor pictures, markings, dark backgrounds and other reproduction issues beyond our control. Because this work is culturally important, we have made it available as a part of our commitment to protecting, preserving and promoting the world's literature. Thank you for your understanding.

Figure Painting

applied to

Architecture

CROWNINSHIELD

FIGURE PAINTING APPLIED TO ARCHITECTURE.

IT might have been more interesting to many of you had I chosen for my text, "Decorative Painting Applied to Architecture" rather than the more specific, "Figure Painting." Not only would the time-limit have necessitated the baldest treatment of the former, but, being somewhat of an enthusiast, I wished to preach a crusade in favor of the latter before those men who, to a very great extent, hold its destinies in their hands. I wished, also, to emphasize the *interesting* qualities of figure-work as compared with all others. Far be it from me to advocate its unprovoked employment under inopportune conditions, but, granted favoring circumstances, there can be no doubt that it offers a mental pabulum much more delicious and desirable than any fret, or scroll, or interlacement, which, however harmonious they may be, at times positively tease the mind. Whether or not the mediæval and Renaissance Italians were, architecturally, as judicious as their more northern or southern brethren, must be decided by my hearers, who are far more competent to settle such vexed questions than a mere decorator. We know, however, that their system of veneering edifices externally and internally with the human figure, painted or sculptured, in glass or mosaic, though doubtless abused, has for centuries rendered them the shrines of the intellectual, lay or professional, and rescued not a few of them from a well-merited oblivion.

It is my purpose this evening, *first*, to give you a very brief historical *résumé* of figure painting as applied to architecture from its inception down to our own times, jumping with alacrity from great epoch to great epoch, noting some of the qualities and characteristics of the foremost men of the greatest epoch, together with the causes that led to their pre-eminence: and, *secondly*, to institute certain comparisons between their paintings and those of modern times, as well as note the causes that differentiate their work from ours. I shall also claim from your courteous patience the right to foist into the body of my discourse whatever irrelevant matter the occasion of the mood of the moment may suggest.

This audience of experts knows pretty well—I may say very well—what Egyptian and Assyrian painters accomplished. In the great days of the monarchy, in the eighteenth century, when architecture culminated, the Egyptian painter was a mere limner of hieroglyphs. Figure-painting was purely didactic or religious, or decorative, or all combined. They tapestried their buildings externally and internally with gayly-colored phalanxes of human beings, aiming for and attaining the effect of a carpet. The course of Egyptian art was entirely exceptional in its character. Up to a certain point it progressed normally; but when it reached a stage rich in future promise; when it seemed to suggest results almost as splendid as the ante-Pheidian art suggested in Greece; when the fair sunset of its archaic period appeared to guarantee a glorious dawn, then its progress was suddenly checked, and that dawn never broke. From the sixth dynasty painting and sculpture were doomed to decadence, only to be regenerated and vitalized by another race and in other times. A naturalistic *must* precede a conventional art. The conventional period is oftentimes prefaced by a mature and brilliant school, as it was in Italy. When convention crystalized the art of Raphael and M. Angelo, it was still luxurious—over-ripe, doubtless, yet not flavorless. But Egyptian art never ripened. Those early statuettes so full of character and feeling promised much, but convention set in too soon. Several potent causes helped to conventionalize it, yet none more than the hieroglyphic nature of their writing. Mural paintings were but little more than colored inscriptions. The art of drawing, as we understand it did not exist. Sculptors reproduced *actual* forms with considerable skill, but they, as well as the painters, were powerless to *feign* forms. The bas-reliefs were as embryonic as the pictures. By reason of the imitative character of his craft the sculptor was far more of a man than the painter. The work of the former was full of strange inconsistencies, replete with quaint medleys of skill and awkwardness. Heads full of character, knees well articulated, arms scientifically muscled, hands and feet only "blocked in," and movement archaically rigid. He worked as the beginner invariably works—modeled the component parts with considerable knowledge (save the hands and feet), but gave no adequate idea of the whole; nor could he express harmonious movement. The development of a nation's art, like a tyro's, can be registered by the treatment of hands, feet, and movement. Compared with the sculptor the painter was but little more than a scribe and sign painter.

Though not germane to the matter in hand it may gratify the *amour propre* of my hearers to learn that neither sculptor nor painter were the peers of the architect; they were merely his servant. The architect, Iritesen, who worked for Menthoutheotep II., tells us that "he held a place at the bottom of the king's heart, and was his joy from morning till night." "The only artists," says M. Perrot, "who had a high, and well-defined social position in ancient Egypt, a country where ranks were as distinctly marked as in China. were the architects or engineers, for they deserve either title, Their names have been preserved to us in hundreds upon their elaborate tombs and inscribed steles." Texts, moreover, prove that the royal architects frequently married the daughters of Pharoah. Egyptian painting may be dismissed with the observation that the process in vogue was *distemper*. The colors were laid on with a glutinous medium, such as honey, or some flexible gum.

To trace the meanderings of architectural figure painting from the valley of the Nile to the Acropolis of Athens would be an arid and sterile journey. Even the Acropolis is barren of results *directly*. We know that the walls of the buildings were decorated with heroic paintings, and it is legitimate to assume, considering the taste of the community, that they would not shame the bas-reliefs of the Parthenon. We can form some idea of their excellence from the mural paintings unearthed at Pompeii and Herculaneum, as well as in the environs of Rome and elsewhere, which were doubtless the handiwork of Greek artists, but Greeks of a decadent epoch. Many of these pictures are admirable, replete with that easy grace and dignity which are the characteristics of classic art. The composition in almost all of them is worthy of unstinted praise and is much superior both to the execution and draughtsmanship, which is attributable to the fact that most of these paintings are merely free renderings of famous prototypes. However great may be their shortcomings, they are eminently decorative and full of style. The forms are simple, free from all accidental superfluities, heroic, statuesque, and therefore suited to monumental art. There should be a touch of sculpture in all monumental painting, to give it the required grandeur, and the indispensable "swing," if I may be permitted the word. It was formerly supposed that the mural paintings of Pompeii and Herculaneum were *encaustic*. Modern research has proved them to be frescoes without doubt. It would be almost sacrilegious to make no mention of the wreath-crowned Polymnia—the so-called "Muse of Cortona," a fragment unearthed in that city early in the last century, and probably one of the most beautiful bits of Greek painting extant, a marvelous specimen of true encaustic. Other examples of encaustic have recently been discovered in the Egyptian tombs—portraits of a late epoch, interesting from their technique, but not comparable to the "Lyric muse." The mention of her likeness would scarcely be relevant in an essay on figure-painting applied to architecture, were there not so great a similarity of treatment between easel and monumental-painting in those days, and the utter absence of it in our own time, an absence I shall signalize later.

After the cataclysm caused by the ruthless inroads of the barbarians we must turn our eyes towards Byzantium to study the course of the arts. True it is that many rude hands executed boorish suggestions of pagan deities in the very bowels of the earth, in the subterranean churches, and dubbed them Saint *this* or Saint *that*, but these hieroglyphic monstrosities are merely the shadow of a shadow, and all the holy zeal of Christian martyrs could lend them neither charm nor nobility, nothing but pathetic *naïveté*. So much for the inspiration of religious fervor.

The Byzantine Court was nothing if not splendid; it inherited a touch of Eastern sumptuousness. It was the day for costly stuffs, jeweled caskets, ivories, all sorts of *objets d'arts*, bronzes, and mosaics. Sculpture was on the decline, and the iconoclasts of the eighth and ninth centuries gave it its *coup de grâce*. It was a great day for mural painting,—for so we must call the mosaics. Even the iconoclast blinked the painted figures, while he smashed the sculptured ones into flinders. The art of Byzantium was at least rich. Supported by tradition and extant masterpieces of the best epochs, its creations, rigid and grotesque at times, were immensely dignified and solemn. Those colossal paintings, effigies of the celestial hierarchy, must have been awe-inspiring indeed to the faithful! Even now they command our veneration. When the money gave out, [everything must have been disrupted during the godless and ever-to-be-regretted sack of Byzantium by the Crusaders in 1204], mosaics gave place to less costly paintings, with which many of the Greek churches were covered from pavement to cupola. This custom still obtains with the painter-monks of Mt. Athos, a monastic colony of Macedonia, where a purely ecclesiastical art alone recalls the past glories of Byzantium.

And now we herald that vital epoch, the Italian Renaissance. But before we speak of the great precursors, we must remember the old adage that "out of nothing nothing is made," and render their due meed to the long-forgotten mosaicists of the twelfth century, since they in a measure prepared the way for their more fortunate and much-lauded successors. At either extremity of Italy, at Venice and in Sicily, Byzantine art, before its final fossilization, said its last splendid word in the language of mosaic. But at Rome— always more or less antagonistic to Byzantine dogma—in the church of St. Maria in Trastevere, the Latin genius began to manifest itself, and the authors of those mosaics dared to break loose from rigid tradition, and take hints from nature. "The twelfth century," says M. Gerspach, "is not sufficiently appreciated; it was a dawn, and it is to the unknown mosaicists of this time that belongs the honor of having paved the way for the first Renaissance. A hundred years before Nicholas of Pisa, still longer before Cimabue and Giotto, the mosaicists created more correctly drawn figures, and broader compositions than those of the first Tuscan masters. Posterity has forgotten their names, it confers its gratitude on the sculptors of Pisa, and on painters of great merit, doubtless, but who in reality have been preceded more than a century by the rude and bold mosaicists."

All mural painters have reverenced Giotto, the great forerunner of modern times. Philosopher as well as painter, this friend of Dante had the power to translate abstract ideas into pictorial language. A keen observer of men and manners he ushered in the dramatic age. Serene immobility had characterized the works of his predecessors. He studied the structural laws of the human body and gave landscape its due importance. His noble and monumental compositions, admirably arranged for the exigencies of architecture were to serve as models for more than a hundred years. We must not for an instant suppose that Giotto was a realist in the modern sense of the word. To us his works often seem strangely stiff and conventional, though always monumental. But men must be estimated comparatively. He was an innovator in the thirteenth century. He vivified the conventional figures of his day. He abandoned the abstract method and observed concrete life, though not pushing realism so far as to make his figures of Christ and the apostles mere portrait studies. In our estimate of Italian and Byzantine art we must never eliminate the ineradicable and ever-present influence of the antique. The rude art of the dark ages drew thence its modicum of inspiration, while to the revivalists of the thirteenth century it suggested statuesque grace and dignity. In the draperies particularly its beneficent influence is felt, to it in a great measure the paintings owe that sculpturesque feeling which I have before insisted is the prime requisite of monumental art.

Orcagna, Giotto's immediate successor, architect, sculptor and painter, one of those learned and versatile practitioners not unfrequent in Renaissance Italy, used to sign his pictures "*Andrea di Cione, sculptor,*" and his sculptures, "*Andrea di Cione, painter,*" for he wished that sculpture should be felt in his painting, and painting in his sculpture.* Like his predecessors, Giotto painted on wet plaster, that is, *a buon fresco*. His easel pictures were executed in distemper. The only difference between the latter and his mural paintings being one of medium. There is no doubt about the methods employed in those days, for Cennino Cennini, who wrote in 1437, has left us detailed statements about everything a painter was required to know, not even ignoring his mode of life. "These were the methods adopted by Giotto, the great master, who had Taddeo Gaddi, his godson, for his disciple for 24 years; his disciple was Agnolo, his son; and I was Agnolo's disciple for 12 years."

You will doubtless have noticed from what has gone before that *fresco* was the universal medium for wall painting, and continued so for many hundred years. It is still successfully employed in Italy, and has been discarded in other countries rather from a want of skillful practitioners than from any sound objection to it as a process. In the days of which we are now speaking, all the painters frescoed—not in the

---

* Lafenestre: *La Peinture Italienne.*

sham modern way—as a matter of course. There was every reason why they should. In the first place it necessitated no delay, inasmuch as the fresh plaster could be attacked at once. Secondly, it cost almost nothing, the colors being merely mixed with water, and thirdly, it was the most direct method possible,—directness being a great desideratum. The more fussy and laborious the preliminaries, the greater the chance that the inspiration will weaken. Moreover, the qualities of this process are eminently light and decorative.

I have spoken elsewhere at length of its relative durability, so that it will suffice for me now to say that Giotto's frescoes in the Arena Chapel at Padua are still in a good state of preservation, nor would it be pertinent for me here to describe this well-known process, which might be employed by any architect for his plain wall-surfaces, were his tone determined at the time of floating the plaster. Its qualities lie between those of water-color and distemper, partaking somewhat of both.

No man can be estimated isolatedly. To form an adequate idea of Giotto's work, aspirations and opportunities we must make a note of his environments, and by Giotto I mean also the men of his time. Italy was just tasting the sweet fruits of liberty. After many formidable struggles the Italian republics had forced the German Empire to recognize their independence. In the first flush of freedom gallantly won, the cities, both confederates and rivals, displayed an almost juvenile activity in their numerous enterprises—religious, educational and commercial. From their very foundation* the two great religious corporations, Dominican preachers and Franciscan mendicants, were resolved to utilize the arts as a means of propagating the faith. Their action had an enormous influence on the painters. "The legend of St. Francis in particular, impregnated with neighborly charity, and love for external nature, seemed to the painters a veritable revelation."

Religious exaltation, however, did not raise all the structures or decorate with figures all the walls. The political

---

* Lafenestre. *La Peinture Italienne.*

spirit was equally active. Enthusiasm for antiquity was in the air. The republics based their politics on classical prototypes and sought to house their governors and legislators in buildings worthy of ancient Rome. Architecture, painting and sculpture went hand in hand. Communal and seignorial palaces, churches, universities, baptisteries, cemeteries were raised as it were by enchantment, and were scarcely roofed in ere the painters erected their stagings to fresco the walls. What opportunities these men had! Nothing else could have kindled the fires of genius. Religion gave the fillip in giving orders. Her instruments may be saints or scoffers. What the Church wants is good painting for her own definite ends. Why! the good "St. Paulinus of Nola" says Müntz, "was forced to make some concessions to the taste of his flock. He was obliged to excuse himself for having ordered the walls of his basilica to be covered with hunting and fishing scenes of a character especially profane. 'It was,' said he, 'out of regard to the multitude of peasants who came there from all parts on the feast of St. Felix.' He hoped that such pictures would claim the attention of these rough men, and deter them from drunkenness and intemperance." No, no! we cannot attribute the artistic excellence of those days to the religious enthusiasm of the artists. Pure ecclesiasticism hopelessly conventionalized both Egyptian and (ultimately) Byzantine art. But the artists owed an immense debt of gratitude to the Church as a patron, though the Church had only a didactic end in view. Nor should we forget the very important part played by the political communities who patronized the arts as liberally as the Church. To cover the walls of their "city-halls" with allegorical figures symbolizing "good" and "bad government" in those naïve times was supposed to exercise a salutary influence on office-holders.

Though the evolution of art is usually a slow and often obscure process, it every now and then takes mighty strides, propelled by the genius of a single individual who not only summarizes the aspirations and faculties of his time, but distinctly adds something to them. Such a man was Massaccio, whom, together with Giotto, the representatives of the greater age to come were fain to consult. Since the death of Giotto in 1337, and for nearly a hundred years the arts had been languishing, apparently retrograding, till this same Massaccio, student of nature and respecter of traditions, inspired new life into their crystallizing forms, and embellished them with that broad, dignified and monumental character, which every visitor to the Carmine at Florence must have noticed. Standing midway twixt Giotto and the great generation he inherits from the one and bequeaths to the other the qualities most prized by decorative figure-painters. Such names as Fra Filippo Lippi, Domenico Ghirlandajo—great frescoer—Signorelli, Perugino, and many others who announce still greater names, must be passed without comment, and we must diagnose the compositions of Lionardo, Raphael, Michael Angelo, del Sarto, Titian, or rather of that generation collectively; for although each had his peculiarities, the same fundamental principle of line, composition and interpretation of nature was observed by all. The flower of art had then attained its fullest expansion, and the ensuing generation was to see its petals fall one by one, as invariably happens when an art climax has been reached. It would be an act of supererogation to describe the religious or political condition of Italy in the early part of the sixteenth century. I will merely observe that while there was no longer that restless building activity which was so general in the early days of the republics, the great ducal families and the semi-pagan pontiffs were sufficiently enterprising and ambitious to develop the latent genius of a band of mighty painters, painters who were fortunate indeed to have been born at such a moment in the development of art. How many gifted men have been nipped by inauspicious time or place! With the exception of Lionardo (astounding genius with an almost preternatural prescience of modern discoveries), and possibly Michael Angelo, these men were but the most excellent exponents of the art of the day. While it is the nature of many critics to gloat dotingly on the past and to decry the present, *per contra*, it is the peculiarity of some iconoclasts to smash the images of dead heroes. Those men were heroes, whose reputations have been established by the consensus of the taste of centuries. Taste is ever fluctuating. Just now such "brushers" as Frans Hals hold the interest of a certain sect, perhaps to retire shortly in favor of some other masters who better represent the prevailing feeling. But men like Lionardo, Michael Angelo, and Raphael have always ranked high. Their *average* is the highest. They have invariably appealed to those who love the beautiful and heroic. They always have been and always will be indispensable models for mural painters. In the first place because their composition is admirably suited to architectural conditions—it is both full and rhythmic. Composition, by the way, is rapidly becoming with our painters a lost art. For ornamental purposes the draughtsmanship of these men is perfection; noble sweeping lines, ample statuesque forms, yet nowise immobile, unblemished by any superfluous accident of detail; an anatomy at once correct and elegant, and draperies as gracefully composed as those of the antique, equally suggesting the underlying forms, but with a flowing breadth that was peculiar to the age. Draperies, like hands and feet, are the shibboleths of a draughtsman. We cannot praise too highly their anatomical methods—mark, I am speaking of ornamental art. The Italians have always been foremost in anatomical research. Artists then vied with surgeons. Michael Angelo and Lionardo handled the scalpel, and personally investigated (which was at that time necessary owing to poverty of appliances) the human structure. But the painters did not abuse their anatomy. They always distilled it in the alembic of art. Note their fine and correct articulations, the insertions of the muscles, and full ample tissues. Everything that was worth knowing about artistic anatomy they knew, and knew, too, how to apply it. Second only in interest to their completed works is the legacy of preparatory studies in *sanguine*, pen-

and-ink, Italian stone, sepia, or black and white on a tinted ground, that they have bequeathed us. For the student there is no more suggestive lesson than an examination of these studies which so clearly reveal the *modus operandi*. No hesitation there, no fumbling with stump or charcoal, but firm, eloquent strokes betraying a consummate knowledge of the human structure and its artistic possibilities. The accidents of the individual—which it is so easy to exaggerate till caricature is reached—are invariably kept subordinate to the type. This is an indispensable canon in monumental art, which I regret to say was abused in subsequent times to the extent of hopeless convention. These studies are always to the point; made for the authors' personal reference, not to exhibit, and are remarkably concise and firm. They are generally executed with some unalterable material, and are as sure as though they had been limned with a red-hot poker. Now that we are on the subject of preparatory studies it occurs to me that I cannot recall a single instance of an elaborately colored preparatory sketch by Raphael or Michael Angelo for their great mural paintings. I cite Raphael and Michael Angelo, because they were highly honored in their own times. Their drawings and pictures were much prized, and most of them are extant to day. Having prepared a general scheme in black and white, they made a series of drawings from the nude and necessary accessories, then tackled the cartoons, which in their turn may have been changed in the final painting—and note that this painting was always executed on the wall itself, not in the studio and fastened up afterwards. Doubtless this was one reason for omitting the preparatory color sketch, inasmuch as the special conditions of the place, conditions too complex to predict with certainty, exacted special harmonies. This omission of an overelaborate preparatory sketch relieved them from an intolerable incubus; for they could bend themselves to the actual state of things without regretting the sacrifice of labor. Highly finished, attractive sketches are modern exigencies, the curse of decorators, and, I believe, of architects. They are costly and unsatisfactory. They commit us to undesirable schemes, and they weary us beyond measure. We come to the final work jaded and "snapless," if I may coin a word, unwilling and unable to bow to the needs of place. Moreover they give undue prominence to schemes that are only attractive as schemes. Plenty of men can turn out pretty sketches who are impotent to turn out a full size working-drawing, and after all the full size drawing is the only thing that concerns us.

I have referred to the composition and drawing of the demigods, now a word or two about their color. There is a general misunderstanding about color which it would be well to correct. All art in a way is a sacrifice. Every artist has, or should have, his particular story to tell. The characteristics that specialize his tale must never be jeopardized by the introduction of disconcerting matter, no matter how great the temptation. If the author yields to this temptation he is lost. The "eclectics" that followed the generation we are now considering attempted to summarize all the virtues—the color of Titian, the grandeur of Michael Angelo, the grace of Raphael, etc., and we know with what fatal result. How many successful painters have had the good sense to perceive that by adopting the color principles of Titian, they must necessarily have sacrificed all the qualities for which they were striving. Although not what the world has been pleased to call "colorists," in justice to them it must be said that they did not want to be. They felt that the splendors of a full palette would detract from what they deemed the more important qualities of form and expression, which could be better pitched in a less distracting, though equally subtle, scheme of "tones." In this respect let it be observed, parenthetically, there is considerable affinity between the frescoists and the modern "Tonists." It must not be inferred, then, that because the palette of the great mural painters was a quiet one, that the color was bad or poor—that mural painter being the best colorist, in the practical sense of the word, whose color is best suited to the conditions of the place. If this exacts low, rich tones, then he should use the Titianesque palette; if light, airy tones, then a corresponding palette. Raphael and Michael Angelo used the tones that were appropriate to the work in hand, and which emphasized their superb and noble forms. They invariably painted mural compositions in fresco, which necessarily kept them in a light, flat key. Sebastian del Piombo, the Venetian, in a spirit of antagonism, attempted the substitution of oil paintings, which miserably perished.

A quality that was especially lauded by writers of the time, and held in high esteem by the painters themselves, was what they termed *invention*—a word that is self-explanatory. Early trained in this direction, and well equipped with the necessary anatomical and artistic knowledge, they had a faculty of grouping figures in well-balanced compositions that seems to us marvelous. They played with the human figure as we play with landscape. Nothing was too difficult. Our compositions bear the impress of labored model-study, or a self-condemning use of photography. Of course they worked on a system, as every mural painter should. Prate as you will about the deleterious effect of a system, but approach the wall in a tentative spirit and see how you will end! A painter may experiment on paper or canvas, or on his preliminary studies for the work, but there must be no hesitation in the final painting.

In the ideal work of art, be it poetry, music, sculpture, or painting, the execution and thought should be coequal; neither should dominate the other, a condition of things rarely to be met with. Doubtless all of you can call to mind works that are more or less unsatisfactory owing to the preponderance of the one or the other quality. In such men as Shakespeare, Milton, Dante, they are to be found in equilibrium, their language giving adequate expression to their thought. So with the painters we are considering. Mentally they saw things beautifully, and their trained hands had the power to depict them. Now that we are speaking of the equilibrium of qualities, look at a photograph of Raphael's "Stanze," or one from Michael Angelo's Sistine vault, and you will observe the very nice balance between nature and convention—just enough individuality to give character to the figures, and just enough convention to lend the dignity and architectural feeling expected in monumental work. This sounds axiomatic, but it is most difficult of observance. Generations of painters have erred either on one side or the other, have been too naturalistic, or too conventional. The adjustment, also, of these paintings to their ultimate purpose was most felicitious, and here we have another difficult problem to solve. Mural paintings must necessarily appeal to the million. Indulge as much as you please in the eccentricities of the brush or palette when executing easel-pictures. Easel-pictures are for individuals as a rule, and those who fancy a particular phase of expressed feeling, purchase it. This sort of art is esoteric. Monumental art should be *exoteric.* The average intelligence must be satisfied and exalted, or the result is nil. The artist has no right to indulge in fanciful idiosyncrasies and then scold his audience for not assimilating them. Such were the visions of the early *cinque cento* men, such the sanity of their genius—genius is never malarious—and so happy their execution that they fulfilled this difficult requirement, without falling into the smooth and mechanical common-place. Again look at the photograph of the Sistine, and you will see how broadly the figures are treated, and at the same time how highly finished they are! They look well both near and far. Breadth means simplicity of surface—not vigorous, and often slovenly brushing, as many seem to imagine. I have before said that a native's or individual's status may be determined by the treatment of the hands, feet, and draperies. To these might be added the infant, or cherub. Midway between the archaic little old men of the first Renaissance, and the pretty little babies of modern times, stand the incomparable inventions of the great generation, of Raphael in particular. The dignity and sweetness of these creations—for they are real creations—are beyond compare. In another vein they are as beautiful as the "Milo," or the young gods and athletes of Attica. Nothing is more offensive in monumental work than the "prettiness" of the baby. No solution of the difficulty could have been happier than Raphael's.

And how did Raphael accomplish such things? I use Raphael's name merely as a typical one, because he, rather than exceptional natures like Lionardo and Michael Angelo, was the embodiment of the best talent of the age, and for the reason that his development was comparatively slow, but equally sure. Admirably endowed by nature he was no infant prodigy. According to his own words in later life he was infinitely painstaking. His early years were passed in the house of his father, one of those artisan-courtiers who were the special product of the times. Giovanni Santi was a good *bourgeois*, who very creditably painted the customary altarpieces, occasionally gilded a wooden candelabrum, decorated processional banners, and probably, when the occasion arose, gave his doors and shutters a coat of color. But this same Giovanni was known at Court, was well acquainted with the literature of the "humanists," and wrote a long poem called the *Rhymed Chronicle*, in honor of the dynasty of Montefeltro. Raphael picked up all the technical crumbs he could in the paternal atelier and then followed the counsels of his fellow-townsman, Timoteo Viti, pupil of Francia, in the meantime having the run of the ducal palace, Laurana's beautiful creation, and all its art treasures. When he outgrew both his father and Timoteo, he betook himself to Perugino, who found in him a deft collaborator. The Umbrian master initiated him into all the mysteries of fresco painting, and imparted to him his graceful, feminine qualities. It was in the Cambio that Raphael first became acquainted with the wall, and, as I have observed, the transition from the easel-picture to the wall was very easy; for the style in both was identical. Nor must we forget how important a part pictorial architecture played in all their performances. It figured as an accessory in almost every picture, and facility in the invention of architectural forms was deemed a *sine qua non* of a painter's baggage. Inasmuch as these forms were then comparatively limited, the step from pictorial to practising architect was natural. When the receptive Raphael had exhausted Perugino he bethought himself of seeing the world, of "going to Paris," so to speak— in other words, of visiting Florence, the artistic center of the world. At 19 he packed up his goods and established himself in the Tuscan capital, where, not putting himself under anyone's control, he absorbed all that was then worth absorbing. Lionardo, Buonarroti, Fra Bartolomeo, all contributed to the formation of his artistic character, which had not yet blossomed. Here he plodded along very quietly for five years, a young man of recognized talent, with plenty of commissions, but not yet hailed a genius. His spurs were won at Rome, whither he was called in 1508, at the age of 25. Such is the brief story of the early career of an apt and gifted young man who was soon to set the world agog. He was the product of the practical atelier life of the time, not of a great governmental school, and when he was thoroughly conversant with all the mechanical processes of his art, to put it familiarly, he went abroad and kept his eyes open, imbibed every worthy idea, and enslaved himself to none.

It is time to bid farewell to the great Italians. After them the course of art moves downward. But I for one am not going to descant on the vulgarities and theatricalities of the Barocco men, which no doubt compare unfavorably with the more contained compositions of former days. Tiepolo, and the like, may be restless and vulgar, but, Heavens! what facility! what *bravura!* We *must* doff our hats to their exhaustless fancies, their endless masqueradings in color, their astounding foreshortenings and perspectives. Blame, if you will, the current taste, but spare the men compared with whom we seem but pigmies.

It is a delicate task to handle modern architectural figure-painting, and a somewhat difficult one; for in the great art-centers of the world it can hardly be said to exist. It is still more or less practiced in modern Italy—*mechanically* with success. Modern times have exalted the easel-picture to the detriment of the wall. Mural figure-painters have yet to endure much before their claims are established. The mental and physical tension, the pliancy of intellect, the constant call upon the inventive faculties, and the comparatively humble remuneration are no great inducements to entice young painters of ability. In fact, the ranks are not now swelling. Many imagine that painters with decorative tendencies can be transferred to the wall. This is not so. I have endeavored to show you that a painter in by-gone days could work with equal facility on easel-picture and wall. To-day all the methods of the atelier are antagonistic to this identity of technique. I firmly believe, and experience daily confirms the belief, that the artist should work *in situ*, and not paint his pictures in the foreign light of his studio and afterwards attach them to the wall. The latter is a false, laborious, and expensive method, which *might* be adopted under certain conditions by a mural painter of great experience. No human being without such experience can possibly foretell the complex conditions of light, distance, and surrounding tone. Modern painters endeavor to express synthetically an impression of what they see—to render objects by a sort of short-hand process. They revel in the broken line, in the vibration of light, in the picturesqueness of life, in the realism of textures, looseness of handling, avoidence rather than the emphasis of form, all of which qualities make him an excellent easel-picture painter and a consummate landscapist, but are positive drawbacks to him as a mural painter, unless they are fortified by a severe course of special study that he cannot obtain in this country and not very easily abroad. While founding their schemes on nature, mural painters must improvise much, and studio painters are taught *not* to improvise. I should not like to convey the impression that we have not made some distinct artistic gains in the pictorial art, but I do mean that the gains are mainly to be placed to the credit of the easel-picture, and that the loss far more than cancels the few benefits that have accrued to monumental painting through modern research. The gain is one of tone-perception—due to an ardent love of nature and the study of Eastern art, as well as to the expansion of our repertory. To this must be added a certain refinement of taste peculiar to the age, possibly to England and America, for French taste is not reproachless. We have also struck new decorative notes which may yet lead to much if we fortify them by proficiency in the monumental qualities. The least our art schools can do is to give an elementary course of architecture to the painters, and of figure-drawing to the architects. Though this in itself will not suffice to create a race of figure mural painters, but it will give to each profession the necessary insight into the other, and avert many mistakes. A move in this direction has been made of late years in the École des Beaux Arts at Paris. In 1873 M. Galland opened a course of decorative composition, which was superseded in 1879 by the simultaneous teaching of the three arts—painting, sculpture, architecture. It is perhaps too soon to look for much in the way of results, but eventually they should be fruitful. One's vanity is always tickled by the discovery of corroborative statements. Before closing my remarks I shall read two short extracts from an article in a recent number of the *Gazette des Beaux Arts*, on the work of M. Galland, which confirm the views here expressed.

"I am one of those," says P. V. Galland, "who, early and wisely trained in the school of subordination, do not admit that absolute independence in the applications of art to the different branches of sumptuary industry, which reigns supreme in the painting of easel-pictures pure and simple. There it has its *raison d' être*, because the subject, isolated by the limits of the frame, is not intended to be united to an *ensemble* of which the elements are associated to form a whole. The picture painter is free; the decorator and the industrial artist are not. In fact the decorative art, which embellishes our monuments by the nobility of its painted and sculptured ornamentation, which enlivens and furnishes our homes, which dignifies all the objects whose use is familiar to us, by charming our eyes with their grace, their elegance, the delicacy and intelligence of their invention, that art which is neither less grand, nor less inspired, nor more facile than the pretended superior art; that art, I say, with *absolutely no* exception, unites all the talents, all the intelligences, and enlists all the productive forces. It exacts the widest range of elements and knowledge, and, in its scope, no part, however small, can be considered insignificant, its role being determineed in the general harmony. The greatest masters have attained the summits of this art, without the least idea of self-depreciation by placing their genius at the service of what the world is pleased to call, nowadays, industrial art. For them, as for us, art is *one*, its applications can be infinitely multiplied, its branches spring from the same trunk, are quickened by the same sap, and are equally luxuriant to their most delicate tips."— *Gazette des Beaux Arts, Juillet*, 1888, p. 17. T. XXXVIII. 2d p.

"Why has the expression, *decorative art*, which was unknown during the most brilliant epochs of art, lately come into use? Did this sort of art never exist before? On the contrary everybody knows that antiquity, the middle ages, the Renaissance, have left us admirable specimens of it. What reason, then, can have determined the public to adopt a new term for an old thing, or why, having done without it for so many years, has it all of a sudden felt the necessity of using it?

"There must be a reason for it; and, in fact, there is one. The adjective 'decorative' added to the word 'art' has been necessitated, because for the last two centuries it has been the custom to circumscribe the sense of the word 'art,' and to reserve it for a special and limited category of works. The fault springs from the régime of corporations and privileges, which has brought about the misunderstanding. Formerly a

painter *decorated* a palace with his compositions, a sculptor carved his marble, wood, or stone images of his invention, whether they were figures for a tomb, or bas-reliefs for the stalls of a cathedral; a potter modeled pieces of ceramic; a goldsmith chiseled the handle of a sword; all that was art, and no one in those days ever thought of classifying it otherwise, of establishing distinctions, of setting up I don't know what hierarchy in these diverse operations, inspired by an identical travail of the brain. Was Raphael less of an artist when he executed the mural decorations of the Vatican or his cartoons for the tapestries, than when he painted the Transfiguration? Was Benvenuto Cellini less of an artist when he chiseled his precious jewels, than when he modeled the Perseus?
* * * * At the beginning of the seventeenth century, the painters and sculptors, banded in an association well stocked with privileges, conceived the idea of monopolizing art for their own advantage. It was then decided that only those should hold the rank and title of artists who painted and sculptured in a particular way. Outside of their circle there should be naught but industry. Thus art was submitted to a *régime*, pruned according to narrow methods, made subservient to arbitrary classifications, and taught by means of formulas.

"If the result had merely been the creation of categories, and a sort of graduated scale of merit, the danger perhaps would have been but slight; unfortunately the consequences were most baneful. By authorizing such puerile and false distinctions in art, everything that constituted the decorative element was systematically excluded from the course of instruction, so that the painters and sculptors when called upon to ornament dwellings, palaces and churches, having forgotten, as being unworthy of them, that essential part of their profession, could only veneer (*plaquer*) the wall with compositions which were decorative but in name. They painted ceilings just as they would have painted easel-pictures and sculptured caryatids just as they would have carved any other figure, instead of executing works whose first condition is to harmonize with the architecture, to respond to a definite purpose, which above all is *decorative!*"—*Gazette des Beaux Arts.* T. XXXVII. p. 106.

In conclusion, let me ask why should not the present prodigious building activity—an activity far surpassing that which gave the necessary fillip to Greek art after the destruction of the Acropolis by Xerxes, or that following the establishment of the Italian republics, and which ushered the first Renaissance—why, I ask, should not this great architectural movement fortify itself with a sister art, and raise a race of mural painters who might prove the peers of the men of 1500.

We have, as a people, one great advantage over foreign competitors, and that is, we are always willing to borrow every new and good idea whatever may be the nationality of the lender.

F. Crowninshield.

Printed by Libri Plureos GmbH in Hamburg, Germany